This Book Is The Private Property Of:

_____

(As You Wish To Be Known In The Oxford Club)

> This book is not intended for general circulation. You are being asked, as a matter of honor, to hold the information in these pages in the strictest of confidence.

"Some men can make funny faces, others can make fools of themselves, others can make money."

— *Bernard Baruch*

In the Bill Of Rights, Is There Any Mention Of Your Right To Wealth?

Does that document say you have an inalienable right to multiply your wealth and protect it from taxation? Inflation? Litigation?

We think not.

The active pursuit and protection of wealth becomes a right only when you make it so. That is the essential truth of our times. It is also the purpose of this book.

You are about to "listen in" on a confidential fireside briefing with three of the "founding fathers" of The Oxford Club.

These are men who've made wealth a constant companion, an inalienable right. Men who have demonstrated an uncanny knack for uncovering the breakthrough investments of tomorrow. Men who've got only one reply to all the punks, greedy lawyers, and money-grubbers out there:

"What's mine, is mine!"

The Oxford Club has chosen to share these insights with you ... because we are hoping that you share our concerns and our priorities on wealth — both the making of it, and the keeping. If you do, then you will surely find this briefing most enlightening.

So let's now join the founders at the Dorchester Hotel in London, where this briefing was held and where an upcoming Club conference will be held. The founders' names, in the order that you will meet them, are Stephen Miller, David Lambert, and Thomas Fielding.

You are about to undertake what may well prove to be *the most memorable* experience of your entire investing career. Check your preconceptions at the door. We are going to cover new ground. Profitable ground.

January 1997

CONTENTS

The dollar has lost 85% of its value in your lifetime. How much more will it lose before you take defensive action?

Why settle for a cat food retirement when people in your same position will be dishing up caviar?

Advanced computer programs now allow scientists to select winning investments with 80% accuracy. Ever done that well?

Invest in today's blue chips for *good* profits; invest in the breakthrough blue chips of tomorrow for *grand* profits (like our 388% star of '96 or our 317% star of '95 or our 1,371% star of '94 or our—well, you get the idea).

Looking to ride the next wave in real estate? Or move to tomorrow's choicest retirement haven?

Clinton's Tax & Spend Steamroller is coming your way. Either you move out of the way or your wealth gets flattened. Get moving with The Oxford Club's Wealth Defense Initiative.

Been putting off estate planning for, say, mañana? Then you'll love the easy Oxford approach to creating a financial fortress.

How to get some of your money out of your country before your country gets it out of you.

AMERICA THE BEATEN-UP

STEPHEN MILLER

Let's begin at the beginning: I love America! It's my home. It has given me everything I have today. I have seen it through several wars, scandals, setbacks, and through it all, I've never stopped believing in America. I would gladly stand up and fight for her again today. But what would I be fighting for? What has America become? Sometimes I'm not sure I know …

It doesn't seem so long ago that kids could play kick-the-can in the streets until well after dark, and no one worried.

I can remember taking a drive into the city for a relaxing day in the park or a new musical. Now I'm met with potholed streets, moral filth, and crazies running loose.

I can also remember when I worked proudly for a hard day's pay and a dollar stretched a long way. Now it seems that everyone's whining or complaining or sitting on their butts expecting a handout. They're all trying to get their hands on the money that a few of us have worked a lifetime to obtain.

Lawyers will sue us for it. The government will tax it away from us. Some punk will take it right out of our pocket.

Perhaps I've grown nostalgic for the good old days. But I'm worried. You and I have become the targets of envy in an envy-driven culture. There are great threats looming over our heads.

DAVID LAMBERT

It was an early recognition of these threats, and a profound sense that our world had changed dramatically, that prompted us to first meet in the harbor of Macao, 20 years ago. Each of us had been educated at fine schools. We had done well in business and in our investments. But, quite frankly, we knew that more would be required.

If we hoped to succeed and rise above the mediocrity we saw all around us, we would have to join forces with like-minded men and women ... and create the tools for securing great quantities of wealth and then protecting that wealth. In short ...

We had to assert our right to wealth.

Toward that end, we founded The Oxford Club under the motto of "good profits in the company of good friends." We have since conducted our business in complete secrecy, adhering to a Code of Confidentiality that has helped us prosper on a grand scale.

THOMAS FIELDING

You may be wondering, *"Why me? Why am I receiving this private briefing?"* The answer is straightforward — we believe that you share our concerns. That you're concerned about the road this country is taking. That you, too, feel the threats to your ability to cultivate wealth. In short, that you're one of us!

In addition, we believe that you have a great many experiences and insights which you can bring to the Club … to the mutual enrichment of us all.

This notion of "mutual protection" is dear to us. It is our lodestar, our guiding principle. We believe we can all advance faster by pooling our talents and resources. We can have greater power and control over our lives and our individual destinies.

These are things we believe.

And to turn these beliefs into a reality, we have over the years developed a vast, global resource base that virtually guarantees our Membership a towering advantage in the eight vital areas of total wealth appreciation:

BUYING POWER

LUXURY RETIREMENT
PERFECT KNOWLEDGE
GRAND PROFITS
PRIVATE PROPERTY
TAX RELIEF
ASSET PROTECTION
TOTAL PRIVACY

Our purpose and very reason for being is to secure these "rights" for our Members. We have no other agenda. No other allegiances or affiliations. Our purpose is singular: To marshal the talents of a global network of business and investment specialists for our Members' benefit.

Let's cut to the chase, then. Here's how it happens:

Phase I — Move Onto Secure Ground

Phase II — Lead To Your Strength

Phase III — Never Ever Accept Losses

This three-phase strategy is currently being used by 66,000 Oxford Club Members to multiply wealth, master every situation, and prosper on a grand scale. We invite you to learn more.

Chapter One

YOUR RIGHT TO BUYING POWER

The dollar has lost 85% of its value in your lifetime. How much more will it lose before you act?

DAVID

All the charts and statistics and sworn testimony before Congress don't say as much about your loss of buying power as this one story.

It goes back to 1970. I'd been teaching at the University since 1963. I got my tenure that year which meant a big raise in salary. I wanted to put the money into something worthwhile. Real estate, I thought. Definitely real estate.

So, there I was, standing in front of a piece of property in Sundance, Utah. It was a great piece of property on a crystal blue trout stream. I wanted that place. Wanted it bad. I figured it could be my little piece of heaven far removed from the anti-war turmoil that had engulfed America.

At the same time that I was looking at the property, so was a Japanese businessman. We both knew that Robert Redford was setting up a

Film Institute there, and that land values would *soon* skyrocket. We both wanted to buy in early. Unfortunately, the property was listed for $100,000 and neither of us could afford it.

Locked out of buying land in your own country.

Time passed. I've made money, so have a lot of Japanese businessmen. Last year I went back to look at other property in Sundance, and coincidentally, so did a Japanese businessman. A similar parcel was now listed for $300,000. While I can afford it now, to me, it's no bargain. I passed on it, and chose to look elsewhere. To the Japanese businessman, however, it was a different matter entirely.

You see, back in 1970, when the asking price was $100,000, the Japanese businessman would have had to round up 35 million yen to buy it. That was the exchange rate at the time. But 25 years later, things are quite different. Although the price for me is $300,000—triple the former asking price, the Japanese man has to pay only 30 million yen. That's the new exchange rate. The price hasn't tripled for him, it has fallen by almost 15%. Even after all the troubles they've had lately in Japan, he has no trouble buying it!

STEPHEN

Yes, the dollar used to be the envy of the world. Its power was unstoppable. But that's all history, now. Now we look out across the waters and see that it's the deutschmark, the Swiss franc, and the yen that rule. That gives these countries a tremendous advantage over us. They enjoy the buying power that we used to enjoy.

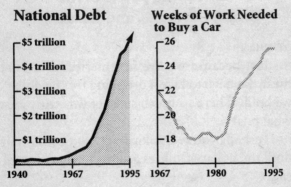

What do these charts have in common?

THOMAS

Another example of our loss of buying power is the number of paychecks it takes for us to buy a car. Twenty years ago, it took the average worker 17-1/2 weeks' worth of paychecks to be able to buy a Ford Mustang. Today, a new Mustang costs 26 weeks of work. The average worker spends two more months on the job to buy the same thing as he could have bought 25 years ago.

DAVID

In the old days, we could have put that two months of income into savings and investments, preparing for the future. What about now?

You can again enjoy the buying power of the Swiss, Germans, and Japanese.

STEPHEN

Just because we live in America, it doesn't mean we have to take a drubbing for the dollars we hold. There's a much smarter way. Any idea what it is?

Perhaps you're thinking that you could wait until the dollar stabilizes against foreign currencies.

If that's what you're thinking, then I'm sorry to burst your bubble, but the dollar is fairly well priced given the sorry state of affairs in Washington. The politicians are spending over $1.80 for every dollar we send them. They're a patsy for every special interest that comes to town. You could say that they're a lot like that gal in *Oklahoma!* who just couldn't say no. Which is why the dollar is going to continue to slide.

The dollar has become a Yankee Doodle Dropout.

DAVID

If you need historical proof of this, look at how drearily the dollar has performed over the last decade. When the Japanese stock market went on a tear, the dollar fell. When the Japanese market plunged, the dollar fell. When Wall Street collapsed in 1987, the dollar fell. When the Dow recovered, the dollar fell. The Berlin Wall tumbled, which should have been a drain on the deutschmark, but the dollar tumbled right along with it. War broke out in the Persian Gulf and guess what happened?

THOMAS

The dollar has lost 85% of its value in our lifetimes. It has lost 25% against the world's major currencies in this decade alone. So it's no wonder that the dollar is no longer seen as a safe haven. It's now viewed as an extension of our down-sliding culture. Which leaves us no choice but to take defensive action.

STEPHEN

There is a simple way to shield yourself from the continued freefall of the dollar. Indeed, you can recover 25% to 50% of the lost value in 12-18 months ... using the three-phase strategy we'll discuss in this briefing.

Our 3-phase strategy can be likened to 3-phase electricity.

DAVID

As you know, in electricity the lowest level is single phase. Most appliances run on this. It's 120 volts with two wires—one hot, one cold. Pretty standard, low-level stuff.

By analogy, most investors have single-phase portfolios. They own what they think is a "hot basket" of mutual funds, stocks, and bonds. But the bulk of their assets is "on ice" in CDs, T-bills, and money market funds.

Add it all up, and the returns are barely keeping pace with inflation. As with electricity, it's low-level stuff.

The thing is, though, you can easily upgrade that portfolio with a minimum of effort and hardly any loss of safety. The next level in electricity is single phase, 220 volts. Here you can run bigger appliances more cost-efficiently. But it's still low-level stuff. Basically, this kind of portfolio would be beefed up with high-yielding international growth stocks and maybe a rental property or a limited partnership deal.

STEPHEN

Twenty years ago, I was happy to upgrade to that level.

DAVID

Yes, it was a good start. But we soon learned the value of upgrading to triple-phase.

As in electricity, you get the most bang from three-phase power.

Triple-phase power is a whole new experience. These are used to run big A/C units, drill presses, that kind of thing. They're extremely cost-efficient and they're also very versatile. By swapping any two of the wires, you can reverse direction. That is, you can turn the motor the other way.

THOMAS

Which is the essential point, right?

DAVID

Absolutely. In investing, it's smart and indeed vital to be able to change course and realign your portfolio on a moment's notice.

You have to be ready to move from one country to another … from one investment to another … from one broker to another … without being locked into one investment course.

And a three-phase investment strategy ensures that you remain flexible. You will never be locked into a loser. You will never be caught off-guard by a whipsawing market. You will be steered safely around the rip-offs and sudden sell-offs that derail the investors who are stuck in single-phase strategies.

Never again settle for platitudes such as "buy low, sell high."

You will, in short, be running on full power, and you'll be unstoppable. You'll be able to seize all the wealth you desire…as you earn good profits in the company of good friends. If you're ready to begin ramping up to full 3-phase power, let's begin. The first step is to move you onto secure ground.

Phase I

Move Onto Secure Ground

THE OXFORD CLUB'S TOP HOLDINGS

1996

Argosy Mining	368%	Semen Grisek	20%
Telebras	56%	Royal Dutch Shell	18%
Lehman Hong Kong	53%	Bank Int'l Settlements	13%
Industrial Holdings	25%	**Yearly Gain**	**79%**

1995

Polyphalt	317%	Siemens	41%
Northway Expl.	146%	Telebras	32%
NYLEX	62%	Semen Grisek	27%
Semen Cibinong	42%	**Yearly Gain**	**95%**

1994

Caledonia Mining	1371%	Holderbank	35%
Argosy Mining	151%	Singapore Airlines	24%
Brazil Fund	53%	CEPA	23%
Telebras	52%	**Yearly Gain**	**244%**

1993

Bank Int'l Settlements	89%	Hoffman La Roche	48%
McCaw Cellular (bond)	77%	Cable and Wireless	42%
Hopewell Holdings	62%	Brazil Fund	25%
Thai Capital Fund	60%	**Yearly Gain**	**58%**

1992

Cifra	64%	Tecogen	46%
Tian An	60%	New England Electric	39%
Hopewell Holdings	56%	Freeport McMoran	38%
Nikkei Put Warrants	53%	**Yearly Gain**	**51%**

Member Profile:
T. S. B. of Missouri
"Quadrupled my money on one pick"

"I've made money in your Mexican funds, CEPA, Hopewell Holdings. I *quadrupled* my money in Hong Kong Shanghai Bank. I read your newsletter every month, several times. I photocopy sections to carry with me and refer to it over and over again. You do the most complete job of laying out your recommendations on a spreadsheet with the loadings, percentages, parameters for buying, taking profits, all that.

"I subscribe to six services but I'm more inclined to go with you all's recommendations because you give the reasons why you picked it and you track it closely every month — most services aren't so attentive to detail. The fact that you are makes the difference!"

Member Profile:
Conrad N. of North Carolina
"Skeptical at first, but not any longer ..."

"I first heard about the club through the mail. It said 'this is the only time we will ever ask you to join.' At first that turned me off. It sounded like your basic negative sell process. But I reread the letter because much of it was new to me. I realized how little I knew about the world, investing money, putting money to work. I found that I liked the Oxford philosophy. Not overly aggressive, concerned as much with wealth preservation. That's me."

Chapter Two

YOUR RIGHT TO LUXURY RETIREMENT

*Why settle for a cat food retirement
when people in your same position
are dishing up caviar?*

THOMAS

I never paid much attention to the need for "being on secure ground" in retirement until a recent conversation I had with my father. He's in his late 70s now, having long ago retired to Florida, and he finally confided his One Big Fear.

My father's only real fear in his retirement years is that "he might have to ask me for money." He worries that he might run through his money before he runs through his life. He has this picture of himself piling all his things into a mule cart and coming to live with me.

If Dad ever needed my help, I'd give it lickety-split. You bet I would. But it would disgrace him to have to ask. It would be an admission of failure. He'd rather have me bragging to my friends about how much money he's still making off his investments.

DAVID

But not too many retirees are bragging these

days. Financial failure is looming over a lot of people's heads. And those who haven't yet seen the writing on the wall are in for a rude awakening.

STEPHEN

Which is why so many so-called Financial Advisors are issuing dire warnings and handing out worksheets to help people figure out the amount of money they'll need to retire "comfortably." But all their drum-banging is for the most part *worthless*.

What good is trying to plan a "comfortable" retirement? If you've worked hard all your life and made wise decisions, you ought to retire in luxury! Let someone else run out of money and get by on cat food, you should be splurging on caviar and jetting off to Cannes when you feel like it! That's The Oxford Club way!

Let's begin to make it happen for you.

We'll steer you safely around today's four big retirement wreckers.

Once you're free and clear of harm's way, then we'll show you the one and only retirement plan that's worth a darn.

THOMAS

Retirement Wrecker #1 is the most obvious—

it's your pension plan. I certainly hope you're not one of the sad millions who think it's going to pay out as much as you were told it would.

DAVID

The average American expects his pension to cover 28% of his retirement, but it's only covering 16% now. Some pension plans haven't even kept up with the cost of living. Others have been gutted by unscrupulous management. It's a blatant crime … but not such a great "sound bite" so it seldom gets the news coverage.

Millions of Americans will run through their money before they run through life.

STEPHEN

People are starting to find out that they'll have to earn $35,000 to $75,000 a year from their investments if they hope to retire "comfortably." Once they learn this shocking news, they panic and run down to their local retirement expert, usually some novice who just started shaving. That sets them up for Retirement Wrecker #2:

They get tied into a "retirement plan" that's so conservative, it doesn't even keep pace with inflation, broker's fees, or administration costs. They lose money just by having money in the plan. Or the plan doesn't take into account all the tax angles you can now work. A recent survey found that 74% of public accountants didn't know all the tax breaks a retired person is entitled to.

DAVID

So you can also lose money by paying taxes you don't need to pay. But The Oxford Club steers you clear of all these problems.

We start by debunking all the silliness that passes for conventional wisdom, and all the self-serving "advice" of the brokers and the financial media. We take these amateurs to task, showing you how foolish, flawed, and flagrantly damaging their advice can be.

Ever made a lot of money reading the financial pages?

THOMAS

We have no grudge with the financial press and the big-name newsletters. Each of us subscribes to several. So do most Club Members. It's good for perspective and whatnot. But we know better than to pay *too close attention* to their investment advice.

We know, for example, that if a story runs in *The Wall Street Journal*, it means that millions of investors are reading it, thousands saw it prepublication, and a few hundred acted on it before the reporter ever got the details.

That makes it as stale as last month's bread.

The trick is to invest the way those few hundred did. To have someone letting you in on the investment secrets while they're still secrets. That's where the Club comes in. Our international network of insiders and experts gets the information long before it ever goes public.

STEPHEN

I'm reminded of how the Club networking concept pays off. Two years ago, one of our Members who's in the diamond business whispered in our ear about a possible "strike" in the Northwest Territories. He phoned our offices and suggested that we take a closer look at Caledonia Mining — before the whole world learned about it.

We dispatched our Research Director to snoop around and sure enough, something was up. Right away, the entire Membership was alerted. Those who acted right away saw the stock of Caledonia zoom from C$.77 to C$11.73 in our first year! That's a mouth-watering, millionaire-making 1,400% profit—and all because of the Club's tight little network of informants.

**Members helping Members
to get to the gains first.**

We score these 14-to-1 returns because we know how to take advantage of superior, advance knowledge. We know better than to wait around until the stories run in the financial media.

STEPHEN

We've found that it takes new Members only a few months "on the inside" before they fully understand that most of what passes for *news* is actually *olds*.

But this next matter, Retirement Wrecker #3, is a tougher nut to crack. It involves interest rates, and it cuts deep for most of us. That's because most of us have planned our retirements on the assumption of increasing interest rates.

DAVID

For years, it seemed to make sense. High interest rates made bonds an easy play. Bonds were turning in 15% to 20% yields like clockwork, and would continue to forever, or so it appeared—once again reminding us that nothing lasts forever. These bonds crashed down and socked investors for 20% to 45% losses in a single year!

THOMAS

Talk of interest rate troubles leads us to Retirement Wrecker #4—a little thing called inflation.

Having a little inflation is like being a little pregnant.

STEPHEN

Inflation is actually on the rise, but the rate of increase is so low that nobody is paying much attention. But even a low 5% real inflation rate (about what we have when you compute it correctly, not the way the politicians do it) means that a $100,000 retirement of today will, by 2012, cost in the ballpark of $250,000!

Let's look at this closer. Let's say you're retiring today at the ripe old age of 65 and that you'll live to be 100. It could happen, you know! How much do you think you'll need just to maintain your lifestyle? You'll need a whopping $8.75 million!

That's a whole lot more than *any of us* has stashed away. And that, ultimately, is why most retirement plans are worthless. As I said earlier, there's only one retirement plan that's worth a darn. It wouldn't work if the whole world found out about it. It addresses all four retirement wreckers. It doesn't involve any cute little worksheets that calculate the exact amount you need to make it to your 80th, 90th, or 100th birthday. None of that poppycock.

No, this plan is as foolproof as it is vital to your future.

This plan is, simply, to earn more from your

investments than you could ever hope to spend in three lifetimes!

Make more money than you could spend in three lifetimes!

How can you make so much? All the tools and knowledge you need are waiting for you in The Oxford Club. The first of these tools may be the most exciting and profitable. It will certainly give you a keen advantage in the buying and selling of investments. It's the subject of the next chapter.

Member Profile:
Burke W. of Maryland
"Made over 100% on your picks"

"Right after becoming a Member, I got on board Caledonia Mining and it has been fantastically successful. I know I've made over 100% even though I'm holding it for the long-term … I'm pleased by all the research the Club does. Not just giving recommendations in a paragraph or two like most newsletters … but laying out the whole story, soup to nuts. I've found this research to be very valuable and persuasive. I also do my own research and if everything looks right to me, I invest. The Club is valuable for steering me in the right direction."

THE OXFORD CLUB'S TOP HOLDINGS

1996

Argosy Mining	368%	Semen Grisek	20%
Telebras	56%	Royal Dutch Shell	18%
Lehman Hong Kong	53%	Bank Int'l Settlements	13%
Ind...			79%
Po...			41%
No...			32%
NY...			27%
Se...			95%

> **1993 HOFFMAN LAROCHE —** Many of our star performers are common household names— making it easy to invest with confidence.

1994

Caledonia Min...		Holderbank	35%
Argosy Mining		...ngapore Airlines	24%
Brazil Fund	53...	...PA	23%
Telebras	52%	...y Gain	244%

1993

Bank Int'l Settlements	89%	**Hoffman La Roche**	**48%**
McCaw Cellular (bond)	77%	Cable and Wireless	42%
Hopewell Holdings	62%	Brazil Fund	25%
Thai Capital Fund	60%	Yearly Gain	58%

1992

Cifra	64%	Tecogen	46%
Tian An	60%	New England Electric	39%
Hopewell Holdings	56%	Freeport McMoran	38%
Nikkei Put Warrants	53%	Yearly Gain	51%

Chapter Three

YOUR RIGHT TO PERFECT KNOWLEDGE

New computer programs allow scientists to select winning investments with 80% accuracy. Ever done that well?

STEPHEN

Earlier, I told you about a tool that will give you an advantage in the buying and selling of investments. It is a tool that allows us to analyze the financial world, to take it apart and see how it works, then put it back together in a way that helps our Members make money. Lots of it.

DAVID

It's a tool that I personally developed, so a little history is in order.

Back when I was a kid, I loved to take things apart. That's pretty typical for boys, I know. But I would put them back together, and make them better, at least most of the time. My mother wasn't always so thrilled about it. Like the time in 1941 when I made a little gas-powered go-cart out of an old tiller we had. I broke my collarbone and almost tore down the tool-shed when it went haywire. Gas rationing and my mother put an end to my go-carting days for a while.

But that love of tinkering, taking things apart and analyzing them, has stuck with me all my life. It's the long and the short of how I became a physics professor and why I wanted to understand the natural order of things, the predictability. About this time, I also got interested in investing. It wasn't too long before I saw an interesting connection between physics and investing.

That "connection" is best illustrated by one of my heroes, Andy Capp, that shaggy little Englishman in the comics. There's a scene where Andy gets asked by the barkeep which he'd choose—money, power, happiness, or seeing the future? Andy chooses "seeing the future." He figures that the power of foresight will make him money; money will bring him power; power will bring him happiness.

Foretell the future and the money will follow.

So I've concentrated all these years on "seeing the future" as accurately as possible. I'm not talking about crystal balls and tea leaves — those are for simpletons and fools, in my book.

I'm talking about a relatively new branch of physics. It began, initially, with my post-graduate work where I studied the writings of Dr. Theodore Modis and Cesare Marchetti of the International Institute of Advanced Systems Analysis, in Austria. They've made break-throughs in the study of natural phenomena known as "invariants." It sounds heady, I know, but anyone can follow it.

A good example of an invariant is the fact that mammals all die at the exact same age. Mice, elephants, humans—we all "die" at about the same point.

Does this sound fishy to you?

It won't when you think about life in terms of heartbeats. All mammals have about a billion heartbeats in us. Mice only live three years, but their little hearts pound away a billion times. Elephants can live for 50 years, and their hearts thump slowly. The human heart is good for about a billion, as well, beaten out over 80 or 90 years.

STEPHEN

Hooray for heartbeats ... but what's the con-nection between these invariants and making money hand over fist?

DAVID

They are inseparable! We physicists are now applying the natural laws of invariants to the commercial world, to product life-cycles, to corporate earnings, to profit projections and the like. We have found that the natural laws, if applied strategically, can make investment forecasts much more reliable.

These natural laws turn investment hunches into thoroughly predictable forecasts.

STEPHEN

These forecasts would have to be "more reliable" by a factor of 10. Most economists are no better than weather forecasters at making accurate predictions.

DAVID

Because economists and weather forecasters are birds of the same feather. They call what they do a science, but it's closer to black magic. They make models. They devise fancy equations. But they are completely dependent on the variables they plug into the computer. Garbage in, garbage out.

Plus, they are trying to predict short-term, which is a thankless business and impossible given the unpredictability of chance events. Physicists go about it differently. We don't allow ourselves to get caught up in the short-term and a thousand different variables. We look at "whole systems" over time.

We believe that the elements in a system will act in a certain invariant way, bringing out the system's fingerprint—its pattern of ups and downs as well as the fundamental laws that govern its past, present, and future. These fingerprints can be mapped with something known as an S-curve.

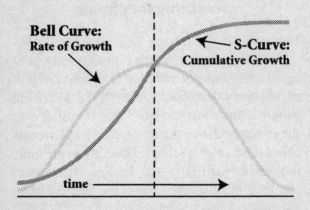

Unlike its cousin, the bell-curve, the S-curve can be of immense value in predicting investment life cycles.

You're familiar with the standard bell curve, right? It depicts probabilities and distributions of events—which is all fine and good. But as investors, we want to know how fast our investments will grow and when they will stop growing. It is the S-curve that gives us this valuable information.

STEPHEN

If I'd never heard of S-curves, and didn't know a thing about their predictive power, I would wonder why the big-time investors don't know about them.

The big-name gurus aren't telling you everything they know.

DAVID

The real money masters do know about S-curves. They use "neural net" computers to generate curves that would make Jayne Mansfield proud. But most investors know nothing of them because the gurus aren't about to talk about them or share them. These gurus are more interested—naturally—in keeping themselves comfortably situated on top of the financial heap.

THOMAS

So let's see what the view *is* like from the top. Compute a few S-curves.

DAVID

You can compute S-curves on any *thing*. On the number of sea voyages men made west before Columbus embarked. On the number of years it will take before the Cubs win the World Series. On anything.

For instance, one of my hobbies is mountain climbing. So for the fun of it, I computed the number of people who can be expected to climb Mt. Whitney in coming years.

To do it, I plugged all the data available on past expeditions into my computer program. I let the computer run all weekend. I came in on Monday to find that when my information input was 95% correct—which is about as reliable as any information gets—then the prediction going out was at least 80% correct.

Eighty percent.

Being able to mathematically forecast *anything* with such accuracy has obvious implications. Of course, there's much more that I'd like to tell you about S-curves and their usefulness to making money. But it all boils down to this:

We can use these S-curves to help us make money on 8 in 10 outings.

STEPHEN

Give us an example. Use the S-curves to tell us what the outlook is for, say, the auto industry.

DAVID

Auto industry? There's a lot of talk about "The Big Comeback of the Big Three" these days. And it's more than just "quality" talk. It is happening.

But, the long-term outlook for the industry is all but locked-in. To show you how and why, let's do an S-curve on transportation in America. Looking back over time, we see a very orderly evolution.

Every 50 to 60 years, the transportation industry has undergone a dramatic shift and everything old has become suddenly new. First, it was the canals and inland waterways that opened up millions of acres of fertile plains to the marketplace. Then the railways that connected coast to coast. Then the interstate highway system that opened cities everywhere. Then the airways that hooked cities to countries to continents in a seamless, global web.

The Rise of Primary Transportation Modes

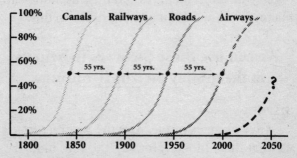

The biggest investment profits are made when the S-curves begin their long tilt upward.

The important thing for the investor to grasp is the "time frames." If you chart these big changes in modes of transportation, you see that they've come along every 50 to 60 years. Once the cycle has been completed, and a new one has begun, most of the big excitement and profit-making from the old cycle has disappeared.

The S-curve for autos was growing at its fastest pace in 1965, not coincidentally parallel-ing the success of the Ford Mustang. But now, the American car makers have seen their best days. The market is 90% saturated. The indus-try has largely become a supplier of replacement cars and parts as well as a distributor of cars made by cheaper companies overseas. There will be no great leaps in domestic production.

STEPHEN

So anything having to do with cars will be a bad investment?

DAVID

Not exactly. There will be pockets of oppor-tunity. But the uptilting growth curve in Amer-ican autos is behind us. In fact, as the chart illus-trates, we have already seen the majority of the big growth in the U.S. airline industry, too.

A new S-curve points the way to tomorrow's profits.

Thomas

The Oxford Club has been researching the next big transportation trend. We've committed our considerable resources to the study of the new millennium. And what we've uncovered may surprise you.

We believe the next great advance in transportation will probably not involve moving *humans*, but moving *matter*.

I'm not talking science fiction, here. This is stuff that cutting-edge companies are working on in Silicon Valley and the Boston Corridor. If you have an interest in the hottest technologies that'll be driving the new millennium, then you're going to love The Oxford Club.

Get a handle on these stocks — while we're still in the early stages of the S-curve — and you'll be bringing home the great returns of the coming years.

Stephen

You've now gotten a feel for the tools we use to move our Members' finances onto secure ground. It's time to move on to the second phase of our power strategy.

Phase II
Lead
To Your
Strength

THE OXFORD CLUB'S TOP HOLDINGS

1996

Argosy Mining	368%	Semen Grisek	20%
Telebras	56%	Royal Dutch Shell	18%
Lehman Kava Kava	53%	Bank Int'l Settlements	13%
Indust			9%

> **1993 BANK OF INTERNATIONAL SETTLEMENTS** — This blue-est of all blue chips, the central banker's bank, is as safe as stock investing gets, and yet it's up 100% since we first recommended it in 1993.

Polyph			31%
Northw			32%
NYLEX			27%
Semen			25%
Caledo			35%
Argosy Minin		Singapore Airlines	24%
Brazil Fund	53%	CEPA	23%
Telebras	52%	Yearly Gain	244%

1993

Bank Int'l Settlements	89%	Hoffman La Roche	48%
McCaw Cellular (bond)	77%	Cable and Wireless	42%
Hopewell Holdings	62%	Brazil Fund	25%
Thai Capital Fund	60%	Yearly Gain	58%

1992

Cifra	64%	Tecogen	46%
Tian An	60%	New England Electric	39%
Hopewell Holdings	56%	Freeport McMoran	38%
Nikkei Put Warrants	53%	Yearly Gain	51%

Member Profile:
Charlie S. of Alabama
"I keep making over 100% returns"

"I took the Club's 1990 trip to Hong Kong and what I learned paid for the trip! We visited the Concord Camera factory. I saw what was going on and I called home and bought 2,000 shares at $2. When I arrived home it had gone to $5. I sold half. It went back down so I bought it again. Then it went to $6 and I sold half of it again. I just sold the last 1,000 shares last year."

Member Profile:
Carol J. of Alaska
"A 230% gain on one stock"

"The information you provide is not available elsewhere. You have things that are often in code in the media. But you make sense. I understand you. That's why I got in early on Caledonia and made 50%. That's why I picked up Hong Kong Shanghai Bank at $30 (it's now $160, a 230% gain)."

Chapter Four

YOUR RIGHT TO GRAND PROFITS

Invest in today's blue chips for good profits;
invest in the breakthrough blue chips
of tomorrow for grand profits.

THOMAS

Here's a name that might ring a bell—Thaddeus Mazujeski. You might know him by his professional name—Teddy Majestic. One of the best professional poker players of all time. Teddy's semi-retired now. He splits his time between his custom-designed, 10-room Swiss chalet in the Rockies ... and traveling the country teaching people to not be afraid of success, to dare to be rich.

The other day, Teddy was telling an Oxford Club gathering why he finally decided to quit the professional circuit. Teddy loves poker. He'll play with anyone, but not for big stakes. He's got a rule about that. He won't play a big stakes game until he's gotten to know you.

As for why he quit, well, a few years ago, one of Teddy's backers approached him with an offer. There was a Brazilian businessman who wanted to play him. For big money.

Teddy refused the challenge at first. His backer kept pressing, however, and then pleading. Finally Teddy gave in. The backer was a friend, after all. The game was set up in a plush hotel in Rio.

Teddy did pretty well for the first three hours. Red chips piled up and then the blue. Then boom! The businessman started playing wildly and threw Teddy's game off kilter. By the end of the evening, the Brazilian had won the big pot.

Teddy was disgusted that he had been wheedled into breaking one of his first rules of the game. It's a rule that he says applies to winning at poker and winning at investing. For that matter, it's a good rule of life.

It's a simple rule, but one that's easy to forget:

You want to win? Know the players in the game!

When the stakes matter, you've got to know the players. Got to know who's holding the cards, and how they intend to play them. That's how you win and then keep on winning.

STEPHEN

The Oxford Club offers you an invitation to the Big Money Game. We know the U.S. and

world markets—we've been playing them for
decades. We have a special facility with the overseas markets. We are, after all, The Oxford Club
with our annual seminars at Oxford University
and 66,000 Members in almost 100 countries.

We also know the major players. We meet
with them often. A few are Members of the
Club, part of our far-flung network. And this
gives us an obvious edge.

DAVID

Now we put this edge to work, making
money *for you*. The money-making begins with
an introduction of the gentleman who brings the
entire Oxford network together for you. He is
the critical link. The captain of our ship. Com-
mand central.

His name is Karim Rahemtulla, and he holds
advanced degrees from more colleges in more
countries than most of us have even visited. His
MBA in finance comes from the prestigious
Crummer Graduate School at Rollins, where
only a handful of boardroom-bound talents are
allowed in. That's not what attracted us most to
him, though.

We particularly liked that Karim has never
been a stockbroker! Instead, he ran a brokerage
firm with five offices and 150 brokers, so he
knows how the business works from the inside

out. That's a much more valuable thing to know.

Before we lured him into the Club, Karim was also running an investment newsletter that boasted one of the most enviable track records in the business. His recommendations there led to a remarkable 30.25% average annual return for four years running — producing such fantastic money-makers as New Age Media Fund (up 37%), Merck (up 60%), Cementos Diamante (up 82%), ATC Environmental (up 420%), Aurora (up 1,200%) to name only a few of dozens of profitable picks.

You may well wonder . . .

How one man can turn in such impressive returns year after year?

After all, as we all know, most advisors are happy to boast a couple of good calls or one good year out of God knows how many. But Karim is known as "Mr. Steady" at our Club headquarters in Baltimore, and I wish I knew his secret!

STEPHEN

I've had the good fortune to know Karim for four years now — ever since he made his first address to the Club at our annual symposium. What impressed me most — and what impressed every Club member I talked to — was the indisputable sense of honor and integrity that he brings to the table.

He has a commitment to his subscribers that goes beyond making profits. Plain fact is, he *hates* losses. He takes them personally. And he's a stickler for detail. Which is why he'll go to the ends of the earth (literally!) to ensure that each recommendation he makes stands the best possible chance of making you money.

When he's not traveling, Karim is forever buried in paperwork — annual reports, economic studies, industry briefings. Recently I visited him at the office to see how things were going.

We never got to speak that day.

Each time I saw him, he was on the phone (speaking French on one occasion, Russian on another) while studying three monitors that beamed data from financial centers around the world, via satellites perched high atop Oxford Club headquarters. It was exhausting to watch him. Finally, I left, thinking it best to leave him to his work.

Later, I saw him at a Club social function, and apologized for having caught him at a bad time. "That's how it is when the markets are open," Karim said with a smile. "I have to be watching the markets every minute of the day . . .

and be ready to relay a buy or sell message instantly."

DAVID

Let's see what investment recommendations Karim has for us today.

(David clicks a remote control and a teleconference screen beams to life. It's the latest in interactive technology. A digital display indicates 1140 hours in Hong Kong. Karim Rahemtulla comes on the screen, and nods to his friends.)

KARIM RAHEMTULLA

Hello, and greetings to our prospective Members. Let me say that I'm very encouraged by the investment recommendations I bring today. Every one is a "controlled risk" play with the potential for fantastic upside gains. Any of these investments could turn $1,000 into $5,000 . . . or $20,000 into $100,000 before the decade's end.

Best of all, these investments meet the comfort levels of people who want to shoot for the big returns but tend to get nervous saddling themselves with the risks you normally have to take on.

Here's an example of the kind of returns I'm forecasting.

A case study of our network of informants at its finest.

This investment came to us from one of our Members. It is similar to our Caledonia Mining bonanza which you probably read about in the financial pages. It's a case where a member "urged" us to look into the quietly unfolding Caledonia story.

We did look into it.

We assured ourselves that it wasn't just another one of those sleazy stock promotions so common to the Canadian markets. And once convinced, we moved in early at $.77 and held on tight for the glacier-sized 1,371% profits that came *in the first year alone.*

Yes, this next stock was similar to our Caledonia bonanza. It hit this year. Again, with a diamond outfit. A company named Argosy Mining had claims on 7.2 million acres in Zimbabwe and Tanzania, right smack in the middle of the "diamond belt." To put this in perspective, only DeBeers has more claims in Africa than this.

Anyway, our contact had reason to believe that the richest diamond pipes in the world would soon be uncovered. This set the stage. Insiders knew that if diamonds were in fact found, all hell would break lose. It'd be "Katy bar the door and Molly tap the keg" because every $5,000 flyer would become $50,000 virtually overnight! But strangely . . .

Nobody jumped on this remarkable opportunity and the stock languished at a measly 40 cents. That was fine with us. We could taste the profits.

We immediately issued a buy order on our 24-hour hotline and published our recommendation in our monthly communiqué. We told Members to prepare for a 200% to 300% windfall at the very least . . .

It's a good thing we acted quickly. Two months later, the hotshots on Wall Street and in the newsletters finally woke up to the potential for Argosy Mining . . .

Argosy soared from 40 cents to C$2.00—a 388% profit.

It was even better than we'd imagined possible! It was another great victory . . . made possible by our far-flung network of informants.

THOMAS

However, a few great picks does not a "track record" make. So let's talk about consistency and dependability.

Let's look back over the Club's investment

record for six years. We could go back all the way into the '80s, but statistically, six years is sufficient for determining how an advisor performs in all kinds of markets — bull, bear, and ostrich.

We'll focus on our top four picks for each of the years. That way, you can get an idea of what to expect from the investment picks Karim will be unveiling here.

(Note: The independent accounting firm of Levin, Zwagil & Block has audited and certified the results for the three year period ending January 1996.)

THE OXFORD CLUB'S TOP HOLDINGS

1996

Argosy Mining	368%	Telebras	56%
Lehman Hong Kong	53%	Industrial Holdings	25%

1995

Polyphalt	317%	Northway Expl.	146%
NYLEX	62%	Semen Cibinong	42%

1994

Caledonia Mining	1371%	Argosy Mining	151%
Brazil Fund	53%	Telebras	52%

1993

Bank Int'l Settlements	89%	McCaw Cellular (bond)	77%
Hopewell Holdings	62%	Thai Capital Fund	60%

1992

Cifra	64%	Tian An	60%
Hopewell Holdings	56%	Nikkei Put Warrants	53%

Throughout the 1990s, we've held to a high 157% return … and we're not slowing down!

Now, granted, these are only our top picks. But that's what we're examining now. And you can see that we've tallied up an extraordinarily impressive average annual gain of 157% over the 1990s. With these kinds of returns going for you, life can get real easy real fast. You've got something you want, it's yours! And that's a very good feeling, indeed. But let's digress for a moment.

Let's look at the Club's *entire* portfolio. That may be an even better barometer of just how well our claims stack up against our press releases.

Take the year 1994. Most stock clubs and newsletters had losing years. The S&P was 3% in the tank. But our *entire* portfolio of stock recommendations returned 48.4% (the power of our contrary nature, exposed!)

Take the year 1993. We were profitable on 32

of 32 picks. And 10 picks — count them, ten — earned our Members 100% profits and higher.

When you look at every pick we've made over the last three years — again, I'm talking our entire stock and mutual fund portfolio — you'll see that we've scored an impressive 31.7% gain. And I want to ask you: Do you know anybody who's done this good over so many years?

This is a rare dependability that we hope you'll appreciate.

And I use that word "appreciate" in both its meanings. Because a few taps on your calculator will show you how gains like these can bring you fantastic wealth in no time at all. Here's what I mean:

Based on our three-year average annual return of 31.7%, a $10,000 portfolio will grow to $39,621 in five years, $156,984 in 10 years, and over $2,464,424 in 20 years.

A $25,000 portfolio will swell to $99,053 in five years ... $392,462 in ten years ... and a staggering $6,161,060 in 20 years.

These are not empty numbers. Not pie-in-the-sky projections. Not the Pollyannaish hopes of an investment promoter. These are the investment profits that are showing up on the statements of our Members on a regular basis.

Audited by independent CPAs.

A matter of public record.

KARIM

Today's list of recommendations is just as powerful and loaded with upside potential. These picks represent our very best thinking and the inside knowledge of our network of informants. Each one has the potential to turn $1,000 into $5,000 . . . or $20,000 into $100,000 before decade's end.

Two chances to play the China Card — one conservative, one speculative.

Our first two recommendations take us directly to the hottest action in the world today. It's our chance to play "the China Card" at the most exciting time since, oh, the 19th century when English traders first exploited the China trade and set the mold for the modern Oxford Club).

On our 10th Annual Far East Financial Expedition in March, we had a chance to learn the truth about what's really going on in China. We saw things the Western media has completely succeeded in missing, mistaking, or miscommunicating. A lot is happening in anticipation of July 1997. To give you an idea, I want to ask you to picture this scene in Hong Kong:

Hundreds of people, even thousands are run-

ning through the streets. Cars are being over-
turned, shops are being looted, armed Chinese
guards are toting AK-47s — shooting first, interro-
gating later. As flames roar through the New
World Harbor View Hotel in Wanchai, foreigners
run to the British Consulate for cover. It's empty.
The guards have left and the massive wrought-iron
doors have been unhinged. The lion has fallen.

Quite a scene. But guess what? None of it
will happen! It's a fantasy dreamed up to sell
newspapers, books, and movies.

The Chinese can't wait
for reunification, to get back to doing
what they do best . . .

Making money. Lots of it. For the last two
decades, Hong Kong has been on a capitalist tear
and lots of people have gotten filthy, dripping
rich. But the uncertainty of July's reunification
has now tossed the markets into a sideways drift
characterized by swallowed hiccups and forced
belches but nothing resembling a trend we can
befriend. And nobody — I MEAN NOBODY!
— really knows what will happen for certain in
July.

If we know anything, we know history and
we know that the Chinese are ruthless capitalists
at heart. And so in all likelihood, once the *sturm*

and *drang* of reunification passes, Hong Kong will pick up the pace. They'll start producing with a vengeance. This is precisely the reason to buy now.

China's GNP Growth vs. U.S. GNP Growth 1978-93

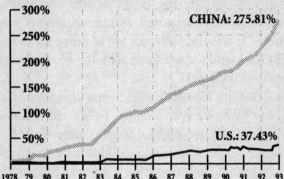

With the Club easing the risk of investing in China, your upside potential is nothing short of staggering!

China is clearly the most undervalued opportunity in the world today. It's a savvy contrarian's dream. They've been vilified by Western media, sanctioned by Western governments, shunned by Western investors. Despite all this, they've been growing 9% a year for the last 18 years! The last time any Western nation showed this type of consistent growth, the horse and buggy was still the principal mode of transportation.

While others pass moral judgments, we'll be scooping up bargains.

Right now, there are a number of solid bargains — strictly the result of the impending uncertainty. We noted as much on our visit there. It was the 10th year we've ventured to the Far East, and we were met with the most "unexpected" scenery.

Out in Chengdu, far from cosmopolitan Hong Kong or even Beijing, we passed couples strolling the late-night sidewalks, dressed to the nines. Alfred Dunhill and Ralph Lauren products glinted from boutique windows. Billboards proclaimed the merits of capitalist goods — from Coca Cola to Mercedes — instead of Chairman Mao propaganda. It could have been Dallas East!

Yes, China is changing! They've surpassed Japan as the country we've got the largest trade surplus with — so that's where the big guns are going to be pointed for many years to come. Investing there *now* puts you at the forefront of the investment community.

It's similar to investing in U.S. stocks back in the 1950s. If you had, you'd now be among the wealthiest 1% of the U.S. population. Your foresight would have created a financial legacy to be treasured for generations. A cool position to be in, right?

Well now you have a new opportunity to use that foresight — and *The Oxford Club* contacts and advance intelligence — to get in on the ground floor once again.

China is about to make a few savvy investors very rich.

We've uncovered two very promising ways to "play" China. The first is conservative and steady. If you're new to overseas investment, this may be the perfect way to test the waters.

It's a mutual fund that holds China's biggest and best-positioned conglomerates. The fund is run by Jardine Fleming — one of Hong Kong's oldest and most respected investment houses. They've got the contacts and experience you need in a region of the world where secrecy, elitism, and networking are accepted modes of business. Plus, the fund is trading at a discount of 7% — so you're ahead from the get-go. You'll cover your transaction costs, guaranteed!

Of course, that alone isn't enough to attract our interest.

We've examined the prospects of each company this fund holds. We've studied balance sheets, earnings forecasts, and the competition.

And being conservative, we're projecting a return of 40% to 55% in the next 24 months — not bad for a solid, conservative fund!

Our second play on China is more speculative…

What if Hong Kong's reunification unleashes the greatest capitalist boom in history?

It's possible. One trip to China will convince you. Over one billion Chinese wake up every morning fully aware of the material possessions they don't have, fully willing to work to change that.

(Kind of like America in the '50s, huh? Only by a multiple of 20!)

And we've found the perfect way to play the Great China Boom for the short-term. Again I must emphasize that this is a speculation. But know this up front: The Club makes it a policy not to take speculative positions unless we've got a pretty good fix on the outcome. Or unless we're expecting high triple digit or even quadruple digit gains. And in this case, we have both.

Let me explain.

When you think of investing, you know that CDs are about the simplest and safest . . . and options and commodities are the wildest with great gains or losses possible. And you know that your own risk tolerance is somewhere in between.

If you're like the average Oxford Club Member . . .

. . . you hold mutual funds, stocks and bonds, and you may have dabbled in options and probably been burned, but you've never purchased an investment known as a warrant. If that's the case, here's a bonehead course in "warrants that don't bite."

In simplest terms, a warrant is a bet on how a stock's going to perform down the road. Buying a warrant on a stock gives you the right to buy the stock itself sometime in the future. Here's an example:

You buy warrants on IBM that expire tomorrow. You pay $4 to get "a $60 strike." Tomorrow comes and the stock closes at $115. Your warrant is worth $115 - $60 = $55. You paid $4, so your profit is $51, or 1,275%. Simple enough?

Well, of course there's a bit more to know.

If you buy a warrant on just one stock, such as IBM, you're at the complete mercy of that one stock's price. Too risky for our tastes. But what if you could buy a warrant on the 30 top blue chips in all kinds of industries in a market that's busting at the seams?

Your risk would be spread out, more evenly distributed, and your odds on success would be significantly higher. Well, that's the situation we have now.

There's a warrant that trades on the American Stock Exchange. It's a two-year warrant on the AMEX Hong Kong 30 index, meaning that in two years you're either swimming in dough or flat out of luck. Of course, you don't have to hold it two years. You can sell at any time, and you can set a stop-loss order to protect you from harm. If a 20% loss is all you can stomach, that's where you set the stop-loss. But here's the beauty of this two-year warrant:

It expires on January 23, 1998 — six months after reunification. And if you believe reunification will trigger a short-term market surge followed by the perhaps the greatest capitalist boom this world has ever seen, then that boom will be six months strong in January 1998 . . .

And your warrant will be worth a small, check that, a LARGE fortune.

HOW LARGE?

That IBM example I gave you earlier? It wasn't just an example. It's close to what we expect from this AMEX warrant. Profits of 1,275% are not out of the question. We're projecting 250% profits at the very minimum. And best of all, you don't have to risk much money to make a lot of money with these warrants. We'll show you why, and we'll keep you current on these warrants (as we do with all our recommended investments) in our monthly communiqués.

STEPHEN

Let me *reemphasize* that warrants aren't for everybody. They're for people who like to get close in to the fireworks. Maybe you'll want to just paper trade these warrants and watch the fireworks from the far shore. That's your choice. But as a Member, you'll *have* that choice.

THOMAS

New Members come to us from all levels of investment experience. Some are armchair investors, others may call us from the futures pits. I take it you're somewhere in between and I want you to know that as a Member, you'll have the luxury of being able to choose from the Club's four investment portfolios — High Growth, Contrarian, Speculative, and Wealth Preservation. All very organized and straightforward.

KARIM

In the High Growth portfolio, for example, you'll find a blue chip stock you can count on for years to come. By way of introduction . . .

Here's a Jeopardy question for you:

More individuals are getting richer faster in *this* country than anywhere else. The question? What is China? What is the USA? Nope. What is Indonesia! *Forbes* has called it "the world's best-kept secret." They've been quietly turning out stellar 6-7% economic growth every year since the 1960s. And when a country is growing by leaps and bounds, we've found that the best investments are also the most boring. As in cement.

Borrrring! Which is why we like it so much. You see, if you follow stocks for a living — believe this, you don't want to be caught dead following a boring industry. But to us . . .

Cement is the "gray jewel" we want to own.

That's because down in the 13,000 islands known as Indonesia, they're building with a vengeance! They're doing what America did in the '60s and '70s and '80s. Roads, apartment complexes, shopping malls, airports. Using billions of metric tons of cement every month. Tons of cement that someone has to supply. Tons of cement that can bring you real, hard profits.

And the great thing is, there is only one cement company in all of Indonesia that's positioned to clean up across the island nation, not just in the capital city of Jakarta. This company rewarded investors with nearly 200% profits over the past two years and they're showing no signs of slowing down. In fact, the stock is now trading at a low 10 times projected earnings. So it's still cheap. And here's a kicker that lets you buy in real low ...

Every few years the political situation in Indonesia gets dicey. Nothing is ever nationalized. Nobody loses their shirt. But the markets fall off ... and that's when we like to buy. We know the markets will come back — they always do within a few short months. And we're looking at 45% to 60% returns on a solid blue chip stock for as far off into the future as the eye can see.

STEPHEN

This "gray jewel" can be acquired with relative ease from U.S. brokers. We're advising Members to buy at our target price for up to 5% of their portfolio. As a new Member, you'll get all the specifics in the free briefing we'll send you. It's titled *Six Breakthrough Blue Chips of Tomorrow,* and it takes you beyond the "good" profits of today's blue chips to the "grand" profits of tomorrow's blue chips.

KARIM

In your introductory briefing, you'll also learn about ...

A company on a non-stop flight to join the world's 100 premier blue chips.

This next stock calls to mind the story of a business traveler in Florida. He may have the world's largest stockpile of frequent flyer miles. He can take an astounding 300 round-trip flights free. He has a whopping six million miles on Delta, and hundreds of thousands on other airlines. He's flown just about everywhere on more than 50 major airlines. So what's his favorite?

Here's a clue: It's the one with the beautiful women in their ads. More to the point, the one that has been posting the highest profits in the industry for the last five years running. While the U.S. airlines have been losing billions, this airline made $931 million in the year ending March 1995 and the best news is still ahead.

They're at the hub of the most vibrant and fast-growing part of the world economy — the Far East. They've got the most efficient airports. They're cornering the home turf. And they're creating strategic alliances with other regional carriers to propel them to the top.

At a time when an airline's stock is closely linked to the age of its fleet, this airline has the world's youngest fleet of planes. And get this: They pay cash for their birds! They've got $2 billion in cold cash, *in the bank,* right now. That gives them incredible leverage in maintaining their market leadership.

And here's the best part about this blue chip investment: Their stock is trading in the $10 territory, at only 12 times earnings, and we're expecting a steady-and-sure lifting action for years to come. Ten years from now it may be flying high among the world's 100 top blue chips. It's possible!

DAVID

You'll get all the fundamentals and technical breakouts on this investment, and all the other investments we've talked about, in your New Member briefing — *Six Breakthrough Blue Chips of Tomorrow.* You'll get the full story in each case, everything you need to invest with confidence. With this free briefing to guide you, your future should be looking up!

STEPHEN

And when you start making real money, you may find yourself shopping for a better neighborhood to be living in, or investing in. That's our next chapter.

Member Profile:
Kenneth H. of Georgia
"$24,000 in new business deals"

"I run the American Institute for Mediation and we train people for careers in corporate debt mediation. We have an $8,000 live training seminar and I put a notice in the club's bulletin that sold three people. So it's not a stretch for me to say that my Membership in The Oxford Club is worth $24,000 a year. Yes, because I'm going to keep running my notice in the bulletin."

Member Profile:
Robert & Lucy P. of Alaska
"Meet other Oxfords at the highest levels"

"Here's an example of the high-caliber people we've met in the Club. We've consulted for many years to top executives at Digital Computer. We were running meetings there and what do you know but we met other Oxford Members there! We find that we do meet a lot of Oxfords. They call us up for coffee or something. It establishes an instant rapport, you know? So much more can be accomplished, and it's more satisfying."

Chapter Five

YOUR RIGHT TO PRIVATE PROPERTY

*Looking to ride the next wave in real estate?
Or to move to tomorrow's choicest
retirement havens?*

STEPHEN

Of all our rights, none is more sacrosanct
than the right to hold private property. Our
Founding Fathers held Life, Liberty, and Property in the highest regard. It was only after bitter
and extended debate that they changed Thomas
Jefferson's wording in the Declaration of Independence to *Life, Liberty,* and the *Pursuit of Happiness.*

We at The Oxford Club prefer Jefferson's earlier version, but who are we to quibble!

DAVID

Most people come to The Oxford Club with
a substantial portfolio. Their net worth is
between $500,000 and $1.5 million. They own
some real estate and may be looking to purchase
another property either in the U.S. or overseas.
For this reason, the Club maintains special list-

ings on hundreds of properties around the world. And we are constantly out researching the choicest properties and white-collar addresses of tomorrow.

We make this information available to Members in our regular briefings, special reports, and "hands-on" field expeditions. In addition, a Member can always call our *Member Services Liaison* and request information on a subject of interest.

Capitalize on a burgeoning white-collar migration.

THOMAS

For real estate investors, it is an exciting time. After several years of sitting in the doldrums, we are now on the cusp of a "localized" real estate boom. Property prices are rebounding in key buying areas. It has been a while since we've seen so many undervalued properties in choice areas. This may be an ideal time to buy and hang on while prices escalate in the next real estate growth market.

DAVID

Additionally, all of America is undergoing a massive internal migration unlike anything we've seen in history. Only this time it's a "white-collar" migration, and the reasons for it are well known.

The suburbs have become pricey, congested, polluted, unsafe and largely unlivable. Millions of people are getting fed up and moving to fairer climates, where the living is easy and property is still affordable. Club Members who make savvy real estate buys at the current market lows can expect values to double by the turn of the century.

STEPHEN

Most people will miss or dismiss this white-collar migration. They will look to buy in the wrong places. They will use old-fashioned yard-sticks. They will rely on the advice of real estate salesmen and money magazines. And that's just fine with us. Because here at The Oxford Club, we know where tomorrow's hottest addresses will be.

We know how computers, faxes, modems, and teleconferencing are reorganizing America. We have been using the tools of the information superhighway for nearly a decade now.

Bottom line—we're investigating the choicest unspoiled havens to invest in or move to. We're looking into prosperous little nooks and crannies along the road less traveled, and we're taking good notes. Our staffs in London, Fort Erie, and Baltimore are compiling all of our findings and making them available to the Membership on an on-going basis.

If you are looking for property that can be counted on to double in desirability and thus profitability, then you owe it to yourself to do some investigating yourself.

We'll tell you what we're uncovering in magical counties with names like Shelby, Alabama ... Douglas, Colorado ... Fayette, Georgia ... Fort Bend, Texas. These are fast-growing pockets of wealth in the U.S. They will be enjoying 20% annual growth in the rest of the 1990s, and real estate investment doesn't get any better.

DAVID

Some people are under the impression that prices in the "plum areas" have been driven up by the last few years of growth.

THOMAS

That's what they told Bob Hope and Bing Crosby before they recorded *Make the San Fernando Valley My Home*, and then quickly bought up every open parcel in the valley. Our country is still growing, not shrinking. People are migrating to places where their hard-earned dollars can still buy a better quality of life.

STEPHEN

Additionally, a number of Club Members have been asking more and more about international dream havens. Many people who have worked hard all their lives and who are now looking for a little slice of retirement heaven can't find it in America—because they worry about the future composition of our country.

These are people who are proud of their national heritage, but they have begun looking at the offshore option. Perhaps you feel the same way ... and are interested in learning more about the living, investment, and retirement opportunities overseas.

If so, then you will be excited to learn more about the Club's profit-seeking junkets.

These profit-seeking junkets will have your eyes popping.

Several times a year, we shove off in search of adventure, exhilaration, and money-making opportunities. Our purpose is a perfectly delightful one—to go to the far ends of the earth if that's what it takes to insure your right to property (and other facets of wealth).

DAVID

In the last decade, Members have taken expeditions to dozens of countries, from China to Chile. We've toured prime real estate, met with local bankers to hammer out financing packages, and locked up lucrative business deals with local entrepreneurs.

As a result of these high-level meetings, a number of our Members have developed their own thriving businesses and retirement getaways in overseas garden paradises.

I recently participated in an expedition to the last frontier of undeveloped splendor in Central America. And I can tell you this, we all returned home buzzing.

This small country on the Atlantic side is far removed from the hustle and hoopla of Costa Rica or the Caribbean islands. Here you'll find a wide range of climates and opportunities. There are deserted white-sand beaches, clear-flowing waterfalls amid ancient Mayan ruins, fishing off the world's longest living barrier reef, bird watching in a rain forest that also supplies an abundant harvest of natural healing plants, and that's only the start.

Amidst it all is an even greater wonder: There are still tremendous buys in real estate. I was so impressed with the values ... I purchased some land on the fragrant shores there. I was able to buy virgin property that I expect to double or even triple in value in the next five to 10 years. There are still gorgeous properties available, properties that are poised for Florida-in-the-'50s style appreciation.

Another exquisite retirement haven in the making.

Half way around the world there's a safe, democratic, English-speaking country that's leading the global free-market revolution. Industry is booming in the cities. But venture out 30 miles into the countryside and you'll have your breath taken away by wide sweeping pastures not so different from the vistas that greeted the early settlers to Kentucky and the like.

This may be one of the last great places on earth. It's in the running for the "retirement choice of tomorrow" with its low cost of living, hardly-felt taxes, and a high quality of health care that'll set your mind at ease. A sizable American expatriate community is already forming there. If you are interested in an overseas haven or a second home, you'll find plenty of guidance coming your way from The Oxford Club.

A Quick Review

We're two-thirds through our power strategy. In Phase I, we showed you how to move onto solid financial footing—by boosting your buying power, steering you clear of retirement wreckers, and perfecting your knowledge of international markets and tomorrow's most critical trends.

Then in Phase II, we showed you how to make the most of your portfolio—capitalizing on breakthrough blue chips and real estate bargains for handsome 40% to 250% and even 1,371% annual profits.

Now you're ready for the all-important third phase of The Oxford Club power strategy. Get ready to learn about the unlimited financial resources we make available to Members.

Phase III
Never Ever Accept Losses

Chapter Six

YOUR RIGHT TO TAX RELIEF

Clinton's Tax & Spend Steamroller is coming your way. Either you move out of the way or your wealth gets flattened. Get moving with The Oxford Club's Wealth Defense Initiative.

DAVID

It's amazing to me to think that the Lord's Prayer has 57 words, the Gettysburg Address has 266 words, the Declaration of Independence has 300 words, and the Federal Tax Code has 12,000 pages!

And if you subscribe to the theory that every word in a federal regulation has an average of 17.5 interest groups defending it to the death, you can quickly calculate that the odds of seeing "meaningful" tax reform in our lifetime is in the ballpark of, oh, say, 1 in 750,000.

THOMAS

Those odds are hardly worth fighting. Why bother? Why get all worked up over tax reform — and one politician's plan versus the other's — when there is a much smarter solution that offers far more immediate satisfaction.

This solution has perhaps been best articulated by Sir Winston Churchill. To misquote him slightly …

> *Never give in. Never give in. Never, never, never. Not to the penny-assed lawyers. Not to the faceless little worms in the bureaucracies. Not to the punks and the snoops who've got snake eyes for your hard-earned wealth.*

STEPHEN

Hear, hear! I'll raise my glass to that. To never ever accepting losses gracefully! This is the third phase of our power strategy and it's vital to us for all the obvious reasons. What's the good in making money if you've got to fork over 40% to 50% to an uncaring Uncle Sam?

THOMAS

It's no good at all! Which is why we've launched our own "tax crusade." As far as we're concerned …

Others can whine about taxes, we're going to win!

DAVID

Speaking for myself, I've got to admit that I used to love doing my taxes. Back before 1986. I love numbers and equations and figuring out the angles. But that's all different now.

I no longer enjoy doing my taxes because there's no longer any rhyme or reason to the tax code. Contradictions abound. You can get in trouble even if you've done nothing wrong. One little slip can trigger an audit that can turn your life upside down for years. It can be abject hell.

STEPHEN

I know, I was audited once, over 20 years ago. That's one of the main reasons we started The Oxford Club in the first place—to ensure that people we cared about would never have to be subjected to the harassment my wife and my children and I endured … month after month … for two years. It was hell. Oh, I won and they ended up owing me money. But it was a hollow victory.

THOMAS

When we founders met in the late '60s in the territory of Macao, there along the Pearl River that had seen so many dashing merchants make their fortunes, we resolved to each make a sizable fortune for ourselves and as important, *keep it!*

We knew that individually we could never hope to beat the IRS at their game, being as how they get to play dealer every hand. But we also knew that if we joined forces with a lot of men and women like ourselves, we would have an ace in the hole.

The Club's "ace in the hole."

This is as ingenious as it was simple and obvious. The goal would be to move the Members of our (then) little club away from the defensive, nervous posture that most people assume ... to an offensive, confident, winning posture. It would be based on the unofficial slogan of the Club that we mentioned up front: *What's mine, is mine!*

DAVID

The tax code may be 12,000 intimidating pages long, but it's also riddled with deductions, exemptions, exclusions and other loopholes that the most powerful tax attorneys are capable of turning to your advantage. The solution, then?

THOMAS

Get those powerful tax attorneys into the Club! Make them Members!

STEPHEN

You probably know that if you could afford a big-name tax attorney on full retainer, you could cut your tax liability to darn near zero while making yourself more invulnerable to audit. You know this, right?

Well, know this:

We've retained dozens of tax pros for our Members' exclusive use.

These are your $300 an hour types, field-tested pros who know the angles. And the moment you join the Club, you will have access to their expertise at a price you'll grow fond of ... *IT'S YOURS FREE WITH MEMBERSHIP!*

THOMAS

You may be wondering how our Club can afford so much high-priced talent and still pay our bills. This part's easy, really.

Our tax pros *want* to be in The Oxford Club! These guys aren't fools. They're quick to see the business value of joining forces and networking with like-minded men and women.

Sure, these guys are some of the best at cutting your taxes in such a way that your return sails from the IRS's in-box to the out-box without raising an eyebrow. But what do they know of international investments ... and privacy programs ... and business dealings? Not much, often.

But as Members of the Club, they get to take advantage of The Oxford Connection. It's a way of "informally connecting" with people in the know. It's the obvious benefit of everyone bringing his bit of genius to the table.

Banking Specialists who take Members on actual tours of overseas banks and assist in the setting up of confidential, numbered accounts.

Privacy Specialists who roam in the nether world of corporate espionage and high-end financial recoveries and who can, on discreet retainer, help other Members with almost any assignment.

Investment Specialists who roam the world in search of new technologies, upstart companies, the best tax-deferred investments, hot initial public offerings, and emerging trends that will shape tomorrow's marketplace.

This is The Oxford Club Connection. Good profits in the company of good friends. The perfect way—indeed the only real way that most of us can ever hope to ensure our right to wealth.

Take advantage of the finest tax lawyers in the land.

DAVID

Over the years, we've used The Oxford Club's tax specialists to shield ourselves from all manner of attack. There must be at least two dozen tax attorneys in the Club today. And their expertise is made available to you, as a Member, with our compliments.

STEPHEN

You will receive regular briefings from our specialists, and you will be invited to meet with them personally at special retreats and in Oxford Club Chapter Meetings in your area. Probably the first thing that'll surprise you about these briefings is the level of candor and clarity.

Our specialists aren't out to win any IRS awards. They're mercenaries. They're trained to ease you through the system without mishap. Whether you own a couple of complex partnerships and overseas holdings, or are simply filing a basic 1040 this year, our tax attorneys will clarify your options in a clear, straightforward manner.

Our pros will explain all the secrets the rich and well-connected use to move through the system ... and slash taxes ... untouched.

Lawyers, creditors, ex-wives... your money is beyond their reach.

When you join The Oxford Club, you will receive a number of briefings on U.S. tax concerns and offshore financial strategies. You will learn how to ...

➤ write-off almost every personal expense using a simple business shell that also lets you sock away an unlimited amount of cash in totally tax-deferred investments

➤ virtually eliminate the risk of being audited by knowing exactly what the IRS computers screen for and what the flunkies are now eye-balling

➤ earn $70,000 in a discreet overseas business and yet never pay a dime in U.S. taxes — this is 100% legal, spelled out in the tax code

➤ slash your property taxes at least 50% using a new strategy that, for reasons completely beyond our understanding, hardly anybody's using

And this is just a start of what's coming your way. As you proceed, you may have questions or concerns. You will again find the Club to be of invaluable assistance. Call your *Member Services Liaison* and ask for help. You'll get exactly what you need to fit your personal financial needs.

THOMAS

Taxes are the most obvious, but not the most odious, attack on your right to wealth. We'll discuss other threats in the next chapter.

THE OXFORD CLUB'S
TOP HOLDINGS

1996

Argosy Mining	368%	Semen Grisek	20%
Telebras	56%	Royal Dutch Shell	18%
Lehman Hong Kong	53%	Bank Int'l Settlements	13%
Industrial Holdings	25%	Yearly Gain	79%

Polypha			1%
Northw			2%
NYLEX			7%
Semen			5%

> **1993 McCaw Cellular** — Our favorite kind of stock; a solid performer that's about to be taken over. When AT&T bought McCaw, we scored.

Caledo			5%
Argosy Mining	15	pore Airlines	24%
Brazil Fund		CEPA	23%
Telebras		Yearly Gain	244%

1993

Bank Int Settlements	89%	Hoffman La Roche	48%
McCaw Cellular (bond)	**77%**	Cable and Wireless	42%
Hopewell Holdings	62%	Brazil Fund	25%
Thai Capital Fund	60%	Yearly Gain	58%

1992

Cifra	64%	Tecogen	46%
Tian An	60%	New England Electric	39%
Hopewell Holdings	56%	Freeport McMoran	38%
Nikkei Put Warrants	53%	Yearly Gain	51%

Chapter Seven

YOUR RIGHT TO ASSET PROTECTION

*Been putting off estate planning
for, say, mañana? You'll love
the "easy Oxford" approach.*

STEPHEN

Many of us would rather talk about a
stranger's prostate than delve into the intricacies
of living wills, family trusts, probate, and the like.
It's understandable.

But it's also the reason so many folks leave all
their years of hard work to the lawyers and the
government. The typical upper-middle-class
family forks over $100,000 — simply because
they don't want to face up to estate planning.

But it doesn't have to be. The Oxford Club
has pioneered an approach to estate planning that
just about 100% eliminates legal hassles. This
approach can be summed up in seven words...

The "Lucky Seven" solution to estate planning hassles.

Just seven words can mean the difference

between an estate that your family appreciates or the lawyers appreciate. These seven words will make more sense to you after you read the following true story of a family that joined the Club *almost* too late.

Gus and Dot, those were the parents' names. They were a typical middle-class couple: three kids, a successful bakery business, a house in the country, a small portfolio of stocks and bonds, all for a net worth of about $1.2 million. The oldest son, an entrepreneur like his parents, planned to take over the family business when the time came. It was a picturebook story.

David

In fact, Gus and Dot got their estate planning off to a perfect start. They drew up an estate plan in the 1970s, leaving everything to each other and eventually to the kids. It was nothing fancy, but it was better than most people do.

Things were still fine in 1982, or so they thought. That's the year they updated their will to take advantage of a new marital deduction. They also looked into long-term care insurance, but it seemed too expensive at the time. They had Medicare, so they figured they could "pass" on the insurance. Finally, they transferred half the interest in the family bakery to their son— since he would be running it soon.

Everything continued along until 1992 when Gus suffered a fatal heart attack. That's when Dot's problems really began. She thought her estate plan was in order and that she wouldn't get hit with estate taxes.

People who haven't updated their wills are in for a rude awakening.

STEPHEN

Unfortunately, though they had updated their will, they left out a crucial clause—the credit shelter clause. It may sound like legalese, but it's easy to understand. It simply means that $600,000 of your estate goes into a trust that is completely exempt from estate taxes. This little mistake would cost the family $192,800 in taxes down the road. But the family had more immediate problems facing them.

Six months after Gus died, Dot had to go into an old-age home. Because she had inherited all of Gus' assets, she was ineligible for any government assistance. The last year of Dot's life cost the family $96,000 for care that should have cost nothing.

The family should have invested a few thousand dollars in an insurance policy that guaranteed adequate old-age care.

Old-age care shouldn't drain the family fortune.

With old-age care costing upwards of $8,000 a month these days, an insurance policy is a "must have." Since so many people are facing this difficult issue today, The Oxford Club has made it a practice to offer timely information on the best options available to you. And don't for a minute think that you can somehow "skate by" without looking into these options, as we see in returning to our story …

The family's problems continued to mount. Most of their assets had been tied up in real estate and in the stock of their bakery. That was a serious mistake.

If they had followed the Club's advice to transfer their assets to the children in a systematic way, things would have gone better.

But as it was, the son had to sell the building the bakery was located in. It was a distress sale, because he had to raise $192,800 practically overnight to pay the estate taxes. He is now renting space, and his fragile business could easily go under.

Adding insult to injury, the children were forced to endure probate because Gus and Dot hadn't taken the one easy step to avoid the expense and hassle of probate. Subsequent lawyers' fees cost the family another 7% of the estate's value.

Add it all up—taxes, the nursing home, the distress sale, and probate costs—the estate of $1.2 million was cut to $800,000 in a few short months. It was at this point that the son joined the Club …

Right away, he learned that the family could have avoided almost all of the hassles and the lost cash with one simple step. All they had to do was form a simple *Family Limited Partnership*. There are also overseas trust plans that aren't much more difficult to set up but which can build an even stronger shield around your wealth for generations to come.

The nest egg was nearly fried in a hot skillet.

It was too late for the son to undo the mistakes of the past, but not too late to plan more wisely for the future. The Club assured him that he would be in good company from here on out. All he had to do was remember those seven magic words:

TRUST THE RESOURCES
OF THE OXFORD CLUB.

That's all you need to do, too. The Club introduces you to the world's finest (and nicest) attorneys—pros who can make sense of estate planning. In the private communiqués, at the Chapter Meetings, and at the annual soiree, these top attorneys can put together problem-proof strategies for you.

DAVID

You might be wondering how the Club can afford all this high-priced legal talent. It's the same way we afford everything else. It's based on the network concept, the buddy system.

We attract the top attorneys because by joining, they're made privy to a world beyond their own expertise. They, too, get the inside line on our international stock plays, overseas banking secrets, tax strategies, and so much more.

THOMAS

It's all an extension of the club motto— "good profits in the company of good friends." And to take you to the next step of this idea, we have assembled a briefing paper for you.

It's titled *Asset Protection Made Easy.* And it will ensure that your wealth remains in your family where it belongs for generations to come.

To receive this briefing as a gift with Membership, please turn to page 125. Or to learn about an even more insidious threat facing you today, turn the page.

THE OXFORD CLUB'S
TOP HOLDINGS

1996

Argosy Mining	368%	Semen Grisek	20%
Telebras	56%	Royal Dutch Shell	18%
Lehman Hong Kong	53%	Bank Int'l Settlements	13%
Industrial Holdings	25%	Yearly Gain	79%

1995

Polyphalt	317%	Siemens	41%
Northway Expl.	146%	Telebras	32%
NYLEX	62%	Semen Grisek	27%
Semen Cibinong	42%	Yearly Gain	95%

1994

Caledonia Mining	**1371%**	Holderbank	35%
Argosy Mining	151%	Singapore Airlines	24%
Brazil Fund	53%	CEPA	23%
Telebras	52%	Yearly Gain	244%

1993

Bank Int'l Settlements			
McCaw Cellular			
Hopewell			
Thai Capital			

**1994 CALEDONIA MINING —
1,371% — what more need we
say? Make sure you're on board
for the next big find!**

Cifra			
Tian An	60%	New England Electric	39%
Hopewell Holdings	56%	Freeport McMoran	38%
Nikkei Put Warrants	53%	Yearly Gain	51%

Chapter Eight

YOUR RIGHT TO TOTAL PRIVACY

*How to get some of your money
out of your country before your country
gets it out of you.*

STEPHEN

I began this briefing by saying that I love America. It was not empty flag waving. In my lifetime, I have seen people survive a Great Depression that toppled most of the world's governments.

We've gone from the horse and buggy to putting men on the moon and bringing them safely home. Today's Americans have fought harder, paid a higher price for freedom, and done more to advance the dignity of all mankind than any people who ever lived. We are an amazing people.

And the way I see it, we can be trusted to make our own decisions about what's best for our families. We can be trusted with a greater share of our earnings. And we don't need some pencil-pushing, Jello-for-brains bean counter to tell us how to run our life.

We hold with Jimmy Durante ...

We believe that government is the servant, not the master; that it was meant to maintain order and protect our borders ... but otherwise, in the words of that noted political philosopher, Jimmy Durante, *"Don't put no constrictions on da people, leave 'em da heck alone."*

That's our philosophy, and we stand by it—tall and proud.

But we know all too well that battalions of bureaucrats and political bafflegabbers are hard at work dreaming up new "constrictions" for us. And we know that the Oklahoma City bombing together with the Unabomber and assorted terrorist threats—as despicable as they are—have spawned something just as ugly: The Feds, bent on taking away more of our freedoms.

So we have to take steps to ensure our legitimate financial privacy. That includes having at least one year's living expenses socked away in a safe overseas bank account—*just to be safe.*

THOMAS

But let's be frank. Most people get nervous about sending money to an offshore bank whose name they can barely pronounce. I know I felt that way 20 years ago, before The Oxford Club.

STEPHEN

It's healthy to be nervous. There are all sorts of overseas programs being offered today; some of them are first rate, but some are downright dangerous. And it doesn't matter how good an overseas program is if you don't completely understand it. It's best to venture overseas slowly, cautiously, using a proven approach that you can feel comfortable with. Let's examine one such approach:

We start with an objective—that is, to set up a simple bank account in a friendly country such as Great Britain or Switzerland.

You will want an account that's safe, liquid, flexible, where you can get personal attention if you need it. You will have to feel completely comfortable—that's the overriding issue. And comfort comes from familiarity, from knowing that your bank will always be there. Always.

A bank is no better than its management. For this reason, the Club has long been impressed with Geneva's Banque Union de Credit. It proved its mettle in our book a few years ago.

Its director, Camille Perusset, did something no normal banker would do: He paid out 150 million Swiss francs to depositors in a single day, as a result of a mistaken bank run. He did it with ease—demonstrating very clearly that he runs a fully liquid bank. No American bank could have done that.

A level of safety you'd never even hope for in an American bank.

In addition to safety, I also look for flexibility and ease of contact. An overseas bank should be willing to bend over backwards to help you preserve and increase your wealth.

It should be able to buy every stock, bond, currency, and precious metal traded anywhere on earth. And you should always be able to deal with top management. The idea of the Swiss banker being aloof and unapproachable is hogwash.

If you have deposits in a good overseas bank, they will make time for you.

STEPHEN

Having said that, which banks can we recommend as a safe haven for a New Member?

THOMAS

There are three or four banks in Switzerland that have a history of treating Members right. New Members looking to store away $20,000 as a warm-up ought to take a close look at Geneva-based Banque Union de Credit. It has been around forever, it's plenty big without appearing to be so, and its staff is first rate. Director Camille Perusset has been in charge since 1971 and is remarkably accessible, welcoming your questions.

In fact, he meets from time to time with Club Members. He explains how recent changes in Swiss banking policy have cut the costs and fees of banking—making it cheaper than it was a decade ago.

He can show you how to structure your account properly so that you pay no Swiss taxes. Or, if you like, you can have our *Member Services Liaison* handle all the nitty-gritty for you.

STEPHEN

It's that kind of personalized attention that I most value. I had expected all kinds of hurdles when I first tried to open an overseas bank account. But I had it all wrong. It was only a bit harder than opening a credit card account—especially when you have the Club guiding you through the process.

THOMAS

To open an account at Perusset's bank or at the bank of your choice, you simply contact the bank by phone or fax and ask for account open-ing papers. We'll give you the direct numbers to dial. Or to make it easier, the Club can handle it for you. We've set up programs with many of the world's safest banks … so we can assist your every step … beginning by faxing your name and address to the bank so they can easily forward the account application papers to you.

That's the kind of simplicity that makes our Club valuable!

You next fill out the forms and send them to the bank. A week or so later, you have your own private account that nobody but you knows about. Then, when it comes time to deposit money in your new account, it's just as easy.

You do it through a correspondent bank. All major foreign banks have correspondent banks in major financial centers around the world. Just ask your bank for a list of its correspondent banks in the States. Choose one you know and trust, then instruct your local bank or broker to wire your money to the correspondent bank.

In actuality, your money never leaves the country. But for all legal intents and purposes, it's safely overseas.

Plus, it's totally private because banks don't report interbank wire transfers. They couldn't even report them if the U.S. government wanted them to.

Trillions of dollars are wired around the world every day—it's too much to follow. I've wired millions over the years and there has never been a paper trail of any kind. It's all very easy and very private.

And to get you started, we've arranged for you to receive yet another special briefing — *Reclaim Your Right to Privacy.* You'll get in-depth tutelage on overseas banking. Plus you'll get much more.

You'll be able to find out if anyone has been snooping around in your private affairs. And you'll learn new strategies for sending sensitive information over public routes with total safety.

This briefing is loaded up with dozens of the best strategies from the Club's privacy experts. Don't be caught off-guard. Get this information.

And why not — it's yours free with a trial membership. Even if you don't remain with the Club, the information is yours to keep.

STEPHEN

You, too, would be wise to strive for this level of asset protection. It is the final step you will take to secure your right to wealth.

Privacy. Prosperity. Tradition.
That's The Oxford Club.

We have taken the time to offer you this private briefing because we believe you will find common cause in The Oxford Club. We believe you are looking for breakthrough investments … asset protection strategies … the camaraderie of good friends … the potential for exciting new business alliances … the tools for mastering every situation and prospering on a grand scale.

If indeed this is what you're looking for, then you can rest assured that it's all in the Club.

As you read on, you will find summary reviews of the services and discreet intelligence sources we make available to Members on an exclusive basis.

You will also learn about our confidential communiqués, upcoming activities, hotline phone number, and investment portfolio with our most recent returns tabulated.

Plus you will receive additional benefits each month in the form of urgent investment bulletins, invitations to regional Chapter Meetings, invitations to luxury pleasure weekends, global profit expeditions, and so much more.

Yes, there is a whole new world of wealth awaiting you.

DAVID

It's a world in which good friends are making good money, watching out for one another, mindful of each other's health and well being. A world in which nobody questions your right to wealth-on-your-terms.

If I could borrow from our friend Steve Allen...

This could be the start of something big!

To help you decide whether The Oxford Club is for you, we've included some comments from a few of our 66,000 Members. These are men and women who've moved their investments onto solid ground ... and made the most of their portfolios ... while vowing to never again accept a loss gracefully.

Each Member has a story to tell:

$10,000 IN TWO WEEKS

"I want to tell you about my experience with The Oxford Club's recommendation to open an account at the Union Bank of Credit in Geneva. It was great to be able to talk directly to manager Camille Perusset—I've done so three times so far. Getting money over there was easy. I got the wire transfer number at Chase Manhattan Bank and it was over there in a jiffy. We put it all in Swiss franc fiduciary deposits. What a great move! I received the report the other day: I've made $10,000 in just two weeks by being in a safe cash instrument."

**Andrew W.
Houston, TX**

INVALUABLE CONTACTS

"I cannot afford not to be a Member. My company has been very successful this year, thanks to a financing contact I made through the Club's Member Information Exchange."

Douglas K.
Topeka, KS

DETAILED EXPLANATIONS

"I am quite frankly impressed. Yours is the only newsletter I have ever received where the editor explains how to actually go about making an investment."

Randolph C.
Edmond, OK

$17,000 IN ONE YEAR

"I've made a lot of money from your recommendations. The two I've most benefited from were ... Hopewell Holdings—I pocketed over $17,000 in one year in profits, and your sell on Japanese stocks two years ago."

Thomas M.
Redding, CA

A GLOBAL NETWORK

"Through a Member I was introduced to in Austria, I found a wonderful job. The Oxford Club has changed my life."

Wolfgang N.
Düsseldorf, Germany

INVESTOR'S ADVOCATE

"You are a real fighter for the rights and benefits of individual and private concerns."

James D.
Pinellas Park, FL

RESEARCH ASSISTANCE

"I have been a Member for several years and one of the reasons I continue to extend my Membership is directly credited to the efficient and expeditious manner in which the staff handles my special requests for research and information."

Steven G.
Kuala Lumpur, Malaysia

FRIENDS AND CONTACTS

"We've been able to develop a number of fine friends and valuable business contacts."

Richard L.
Palm Beach, FL

PERSONAL ASSISTANCE

"Dear Research Department: You have always answered my questions in simple terms and given the needed information. It's a pleasure to work with you."

William D.
Louisville, KY

GLOBAL PROFIT TAKING

"I've made lots of money on your Latin America investment picks … thank you."

Roger B.
Costa Mesa, CA

PROFITABLE INVESTMENT TOURS

"You do a tremendous job arranging investment tours. They provide a unique perspective and are always informative and provide valuable contacts. We have profited nicely."

Wallace E.
New York, NY

The Oxford Club maintains strict privacy for its Members. We do not rent or sell Members' names to outside organizations and we will only use their last names in our written materials upon approval. We certify that the individuals quoted in this report are real (an uncommon practice, we know). In fact, it's quite possible that you might be sitting next to one at the next Oxford Club meeting!

The Oxford Club isn't for everyone. If it is for you, then the best is still to come.

THE OXFORD CLUB'S TOP HOLDINGS

1996

Argosy Mining	368%	Semen Grisek	20%
Telebras	56%	Royal Dutch Shell	18%
Lehman Hong Kong	53%	Bank Int'l Settlements	13%
Industrial Holdings	25%	**Yearly Gain**	**79%**

1995

Polyphalt	317%	Telebras	32%
Northway Expl.	146%	Semen Grisek	27%
NYLEX	62%	Bank Int'l Settlements	27%
Semen Cibinong	42%	Royal Dutch Shell	25%
Siemens	41%	**Yearly Gain**	**80%**

1994

Caledonia Mining	1371%	Singapore Airlines	24%
Argosy Mining	151%	CEPA	23%
Brazil Fund	53%	Nestlé	12%
Telebras	52%	STET	9%
Holderbank	35%	**Yearly Gain**	**192%**

1993

Bank Int'l Settlements	89%	Cable and Wireless	42%
McCaw Cellular (bond)	77%	Brazil Fund	25%
Hopewell Holdings	62%	Latin Amer. Inv. Fund	17%
Thai Capital Fund	60%	Southwest Bell	13%
Hoffman La Roche	48%	**Yearly Gain**	**48%**

1992

Cifra	64%	New England Electric	39%
Tian An	60%	Freeport McMoran	38%
Hopewell Holdings	56%	Asia Pacific Fund	21%
Nikkei Put Warrants	53%	Banacci	20%
Tecogen	46%	**Yearly Gain**	**44%**

The Oxford Club has averaged 91% returns on its top holdings over 4 years. But not every member invests in every top holding. So we've charted the effect of a single $5,000 investment at a 33% return— which is all but inevitable for a savvy new member of The Oxford Club.

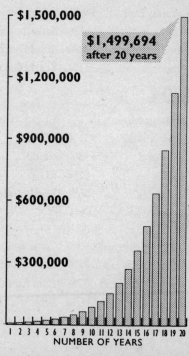

$1,499,694
after 20 years

NUMBER OF YEARS

COULD YOU USE A "GILDED" ROLODEX?

Imagine walking into a corner market in one of the world's classiest neighborhoods and taking a look at the bulletin board. All kinds of listings would be posted. A whole new world of opportunities would open up to you.

Well, imagine no more. As an Oxford Club Member, you will have access to our monthly bulletin board and Webpage, allowing you to tap into a global network of exclusive contacts. You can submit your own personal or business announcements free of charge. Below are some recent announcements.

Note: We have edited these listings to more quickly communicate the offering.

FINANCING AVAILABLE — Offering $50,000 and up for new/existing businesses, commercial real estate. Low fees and fast, professional service.

TRAVEL COMPANION — Bilingual European lady seeks to serve as a travel companion in exchange for expenses.

IMPORT/EXPORT CONTACT — Importer is interested in communicating with other Members in the business to establish mutually beneficial relationships.

FREE ADVERTISING — Members may advertise in any one of three widely-distributed and well-read international sales/marketing directories.

COCKTAIL PARTY — For our Oxford Club friends in the Philadelphia area, we're hosting a social gathering at our home.

SCHOLARSHIP MONEY — Member has a proprietary database of 200,000 scholarship money sources. Will tailor to your student's needs/desires.

TRAVEL LOVERS — Save money and earn commissions on every trip you take. This is not a travel club; it's an offer to Oxford Club Members only.

A "HEALTH FOR LIFE" PROGRAM — Members receive a 15% discount at a state-of-the-art health and rejuvenation spa near Cancun.

REAL ESTATE IN OREGON

A dream retirement property on a gorgeous stretch of the Umpqua. Excellent way to play the real estate turnaround.

Whether you have property for sale, need venture capital, want a travel companion, or whatever your desire—you will find a "gilded rolodex" included in each Oxford Club communiqué.

What can you expect immediately upon joining The Oxford Club? Read on …

MORE BENEFITS OF OXFORD CLUB MEMBERSHIP

THE EXCLUSIVE OXFORD CLUB LIBRARY
(Value: $125)

The Club maintains a world-class library of Executive Briefings on a myriad of subjects. You can receive up to 5 free gifts right away:

➤ *Six Breakthrough Blue Chips of Tomorrow*

Our six top recommendations at this time, each a blue chip in the making, including:

Southeast Asia's largest bank — riding the great Thailand export boom so well, it's the second most profitable bank on earth … and rising!

A small U.S. rivet company that's about to corner the boring little "industrial parts" industry and rack up 180% gains in the next three years doing it!

The phone company in South America that's angling to become the next Telefonos de Mexico success story — and we think they've got the right stuff!

➤ *Asset Protection Made Easy*

We're all under attack from governmental restrictions, confiscations, litigations. And now we've pioneered an easy way to secure your wealth:

How to set up a foreign trust that nobody

can bust.

Why Nevada is America's corporate home of choice — and why you should consider it, too.

How a Family Limited Partnership can save you taxes, protect your holdings, and distribute income at the lowest possible tax rates.

➤ *Double Your Cash, Lower Your Risk*

If you're settling for 4% to 8% returns on the monthly income checks you depend on, then you're settling for 50% to 100% less than our Club Members demand and get — without taking on any additional risk! Find out about a steady 12% bond fund, a solid 9.1% preferred issue, and more. This stuff's guaranteed safe, look into it!

➤ *Reclaim Your Right to Privacy*

Join us for two years and receive top advice from our security experts on vital concerns —

How you can still transfer assets offshore quietly, confidentially, and with no IRS reporting required!

How to easily find out who's been checking on you lately.

How to send sensitive information over public routes with total safety and all kinds of other key safeguards for living in our "not so private" times.

➤ *Time to Take Your Retirement Money and Run?*

You must respond within 10 days to receive this special briefing. New laws make it possible for you to cash-out of your retirement fund and *not* pay the 15% penalty. And why would you want to pull out early? There's a good chance the government will steal back some of the tax benefits of retirement plans in a desperate attempt to squeeze more tax revenue out of us. Right now you have a limited window to act. Get the details!

MONTHLY COMMUNIQUÉS
(Value: $150)

Your first monthly communiqué may surprise you. This 12-page gem is not crammed with advice. It contains only one or two astoundingly profitable strategies, explained in painstaking detail so you have everything you need to make a safe, intelligent decision. With your first communiqué, you will also receive our current investment portfolio, our bylaws, rules on privacy, personal passcard, and more ...

MEMBER SERVICES LIAISON
(Value: $250)

When the communiqués and executive briefings aren't enough, you have an entire research department to access. These pros can answer just about any question or fill any request. They can help you open an overseas bank account, make a business contact, run a computer search—you name it. Your own research team is only a phone call away.

SAVE ON BROKERAGE COMMISSIONS
(Value: $150 to $1,500)

Over the years we've collected a handful of brokers who can be trusted to deliver exceptional service for the lowest price. When you join, you'll receive a list of talented brokers who offer full service at lower-than-discount commissions.

CONFIDENTIAL TELEPHONE ALERT
(Value: $100)

Communiqués, briefings, personal assistance, what more can we do for our Members? Plenty! Members are given a confidential phone number to call—at any time—to receive critical advice on the status of the markets and the Club's investment portfolio.

THE PRIZED BLUE BOOK
(Invaluable)

This 180-page directory is a virtual "Who's Who" of 20th Century Talent. You'll find the "vitals" on the financial wizards of our time, as well as artists, academics, and businessmen in nearly every field of endeavor. Yes, this is the Members' roster (and Members who wish to be included must submit a permission form). People have been known to join the Club merely to get their hands on "the blue book." We trust that your motives are more pure of heart.

ANNUAL GALA RECEPTION
(Invaluable)

This black-tie optional party is your official welcome to The Oxford Club, and every year it gets better. We never know what Executive Director Julia Guth is planning. Only one thing is certain. You will meet extraordinary people, make lasting friendships, and take home fond memories and valuable business cards.

PROFITEERING EXPEDITIONS
(Invaluable)

The take-charge spirit of The Oxford Club's founders is abundantly alive in our global financial tours. The aim is to have a rollicking good time and to come back with the goods. On the latest trip to New Zealand, we uncovered prime investment property and cut business deals. Where will the Club go next? Wherever the world's biggest profits await!

URGENT INVESTMENT BULLETINS
(Value: $75)

The global markets never sleep. If your investments are about to light up, or burn out, you want to know beforehand. Or if our agents uncover a hot opportunity, you want in before the crowd. We make it happen by rushing you an express mail message. It will be short and sweet, preparing you to take decisive action.

MEMBERS' EXCHANGE
(Value: $100)

Here's your chance to make a personal announcement, offer a valuable service, ask for a travel buddy, whatever your heart's desire. Our Members' Exchange may be the most exclusive "bulletin board" in the world. And now you can use it to uncover a gold mine of contacts and opportunities you simply cannot find anywhere else.

REGIONAL CHAPTER ACTIVITIES
(Value: $300-1,000)

Making friends and business contacts with Club Members in your area is only half the reason to attend. You can also meet with the world's top investment, legal, and tax experts in the convenience of your hometown area. Seminars like these normally cost $295 to $995, but they are yet another free benefit of Membership.

THE OXFORD CLUBHOUSE
(INVALUABLE)

When your travels bring you to Baltimore or Washington, DC, we invite you to visit the Club's headquarters — a richly appointed, pre-Civil War mansion set like a jewel in the historic Mt. Vernon District of Baltimore.

OXFORD STUDY FELLOWSHIP
(Invaluable)

Where better to further your education than at the world's center of higher education, Oxford University? Members gather with a distinguished post-graduate faculty for four days of instruction and private consultation in Advanced Wealth Protection. A tour through Old England makes an enchanting complement to this invaluable, life-benefiting program.

**And oh how you benefit!
Turn the page and allow us to "toast"
our success together.**

97 LEVELS OF WEALTH
AND WELL BEING

As an Oxford Club Member, you will prosper in so many ways — in your outlook on the world, in your approach to travel, in the wealth you obtain and learn to safeguard.

Here is a summary of the 97 levels of wealth and well being that will come your way in the months and years ahead.

1. You will enjoy good profits in the company of good friends.

2. You will be the first into stocks like Caledonia Mining—up 1,540% in its first year.

3. You will probably become a millionaire (if you aren't now).

4. You won't give a hoot about who's running the show in Washington—you'll be sitting pretty above it all.

5. Your money will be invested in safe offshore havens — within *your* easy reach, out of everyone else's reach.

6. You will be invited to Oxford University for

advanced tutelage.

7. You'll spend hours with the Club Directory, planning ventures with fellow Members.

8-12. You will pick up five strategies for building wealth tax-free.

13. You will be given a specific strategy to counter Clinton's planned tax attacks on small business.

14-19. You will use *The Oxford Club's Six Pillars of Wealth* to become financially independent.

20-25. You will have an opportunity to profit from The Six Breakthrough Blue Chips of Tomorrow.

26. You will turn your broker from an enemy to an ally (which is better than outright despising him, anyway).

27-30. You will learn four strategies for taking profits; in fact, you will spend considerable time taking profits.

31. You will set up asset protection plans without all the legal hassles.

32-38. You just might find yourself retiring to Belize, New Zealand, or one of the seven other overseas Edens the Oxford Club has scoped out for Members exclusively!

39. Unless you request otherwise, you'll be contacted from time to time by fellow Members with lucrative business propositions.

40-41. You will learn two ingenious plans (used by high rollers around the world) to borrow money privately.

42. You will have an investor's advocate on your side, steering you clear of scams and fraudulent schemes.

43. You may obtain an offshore credit card that you can use to make purchases of up to $10,000 without reporting it to the IRS.

44. You will be among an elite few who recognize and profit from the emerging trends of 1997, 1998, 1999, well, you get the idea.

45-48. You will learn about four great sideline businesses that are perfect for a housewife or a "semi-retired" couple.

49. You will receive free special reports such as *The Oxford Club's Guide to Reliable Bankers and Brokers*.

50. You will travel creatively, and ambitiously; your every weekend jaunt could become a tax-free business junket.

51-60. You'll be given ten sure-fire tips and insider sources to help you raise venture capital.

61. You will hook into a clearinghouse of new inventions and business ideas.

62. You will learn about offshore maildrops, and how they could save your business from legal disaster.

63. You will meet so many successful investors that winning habits will automatically rub off on you.

64. You will pay far less in taxes. Far less.

65. You will see your business grow in leaps and bounds when you begin using the Club's extraordinary referral sources.

66. You will say *sayonara* to incompetent lawyers— you will be judgment proof, your assets impenetrable, your good name untouchable.

67. Whatever your financial interests—stocks, bonds, real estate, commodities, precious metals, you will have a Member Services Liaison

to help you make wise moves.

68. You will receive an annual survey of precious-metals dealers—insuring the highest quality at the lowest price.

69. You will learn the most effective way to privately transfer cash offshore.

70. You will never again sweat the complicated insurance game.

71. You will be briefed on an advanced international strategy for cutting your mortgage interest *significantly*.

72. You will be updated on the growing abuse and fraud in pension plans — so you don't fall victim.

73-78. You will learn the six key steps to take in any dangerous situation to protect yourself and your loved ones.

79. You will cut your chances of facing a tax audit almost to zero!

80. You will learn how your company can be used to deduct your spouse's medical bills.

81-88. The eight top Swiss Money Strategies will

become second nature to you.

89. Your eyes will be opened to new investment vistas — such as "warrants" that can turn $10,000 into $30,000 in two weeks' time. Risky? A little. But we show you how to guarantee against loss.

90. You will get the inside line on auction news, wine purchases and other fine aspects of good living.

91. Your "safe money" will be earning 100% to 200% more than CDs or bank deposits.

92. You will become less reliant on slow-poke U.S news sources, ensuring that your foreign holdings are always safe and sound.

93. You will be briefed on an FDIC-insured checking account that pays a high 6.2% interest rate when others are settling for 1% to 2% tops.

94. You will enjoy substantial Member discounts in your travels.

95. You will turn your hobby into a grand-slam enterprise—a tax-deductible, profit-generating, rollicking good time.

96. You will create a legacy of private wealth —
    something your heirs will appreciate and
    honor for generations.

97. And lastly, you will be joining a Club that's
    good enough for you. Welcome!

   There you have it, 97 levels of wealth and
well being. We chose the number 97 for good
reason. It is intended to show you how remark-
ably profitable the Oxford Club can be for you:
You see, during this trial nominating period, the
Club's Annual Dues of $150 are being waived
and you need only pay the Club's Trial Fee of
$97. Each of the above benefits is yours, then, for
$1 apiece. We can't imagine a better deal. So go
ahead and choose the course of your future.

   This Could Be The Start of Something Big!